What's in this book

This book belongs to

_____

美食节 Food festival

学习内容 Contents

沟通 Communication

说说食物和饮料
Talk about food and drinks

★ 面条	noodle
★ 面包	bread
★ 汽水	soft drink
★ 杯子	cup, glass
★ 渴	thirsty
★ 汤	soup
★ 冰箱	refrigerator
★ 都	all
筷子	chopsticks
炒饭	fried rice
饺子	dumpling
准备	to prepare
餐馆	restaurant
欢迎	to welcome
碗	bowl

句式 Sentence patterns

同学们都准备了不同的美食。
Schoolmates all prepared different kinds of food.

这些都是我爸爸做的。
These all were made by my father.

跨学科学习 Project

认识五种基本味道，并尝味道，猜食物
Learn the five basic tastes and try the blindfolded taste test

文化 Cultures

中式就餐礼仪
Chinese dining etiquette

Get ready

1 Has your school ever held a food festival?

2 What is your favourite food?

3 What food can you see here?

zhǔn bèi
准备

dōu
都

今天，学校举行美食节，同学们都准备了不同的美食。

伊森和艾文拿着面包和汽水，说：
"欢迎大家来我们的餐馆！"

jiǎo zi
饺子

miàn tiáo
面条

玲玲准备了面条和饺子，爱莎看见了，说："你的食物应该很好吃！"

tāng
汤

chǎo fàn
炒饭

"你们试试炒饭和蔬菜汤，这些都是
我爸爸做的。"爱莎又说。

浩浩说：“你们渴吗？喝我做的果汁吧！果汁在冰箱里面，很新鲜。”

"这里只有碗、刀、叉、筷子和盘子，谁带了杯子？"伊森问。哎呀，大家都忘了！

Let's think

1 Recall the story. Match the food prepared by the children.

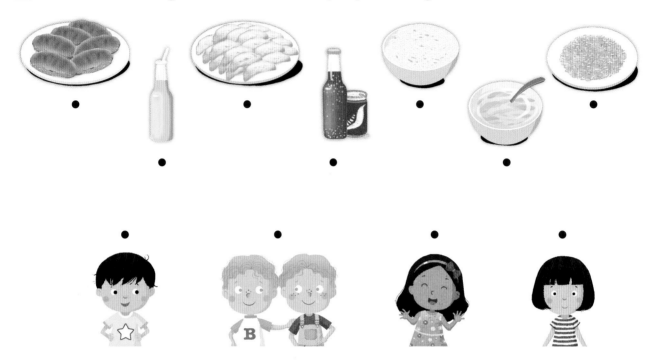

2 What will you prepare if your school holds a food festival? Draw your ideas below and tell your friend.

我要做……

我和妈妈一起准备蔬菜水果汁。

我和妈妈做蛋糕。

New words

1 Learn the new words.

2 Point to the above words randomly and ask your friend to say them.

听听说说 Listen and say

 1 Listen and circle the correct letters.

1 男孩要了什么果汁?

a 葡萄汁

b 苹果汁

c 香蕉汁

2 男孩还要了什么?

a 炒饭

b 饺子

c 蔬菜汤

3 男孩没有要什么?

a 面条

b 面包

c 汉堡包

2 Look at the pictures. Listen to the story a

① 跑步真累! 我饿了, 我们一起去吃午饭吧。

太好了! 因为我也饿了。

③ 这些食物都不健康。你别天天吃。

那我们吃什么?

你想吃什么?

我想吃汉堡包和薯条,喝汽水。

我们去公园北边的中国餐馆吧,那里的饺子和面条都很好吃。

好啊,我们快走吧!

3 Complete the sentences and role-play with your friend.

| a 筷子 | b 面包 | c 都 |
| d 碗 | e 冰箱 | f 渴 |

你___吗?家里没有汽水,只有果汁,在___里。

___和蔬菜汤,我___很喜欢。

快来吃晚饭吧,面条在___里,___也准备好了。

Task

Draw and tell your friend what you ate yesterday.

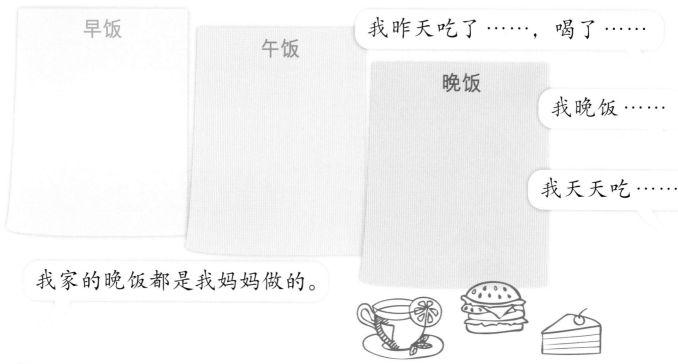

我昨天吃了……，喝了……

我晚饭……

我天天吃……

我家的晚饭都是我妈妈做的。

Game

Find and circle food words. Play with your friend to see who can circle the most food words.

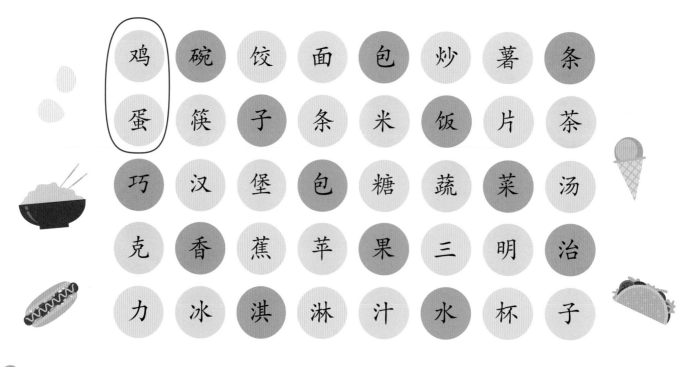

Chant

Listen and say.

我准备炒饭，
你准备饺子，
他准备面条，
她准备面包。
今天学校美食节，
大家都带来美食。

我爱吃炒饭，
你爱吃饺子，
他爱吃面条，
她爱吃面包。
大家都爱喝果汁，
大家都爱蔬菜汤。

生活用语 Daily expressions

欢迎你来学校！
Welcome to our school!

准备一下。
Getting ready.

写一写 Write

1 Trace and write the characters.

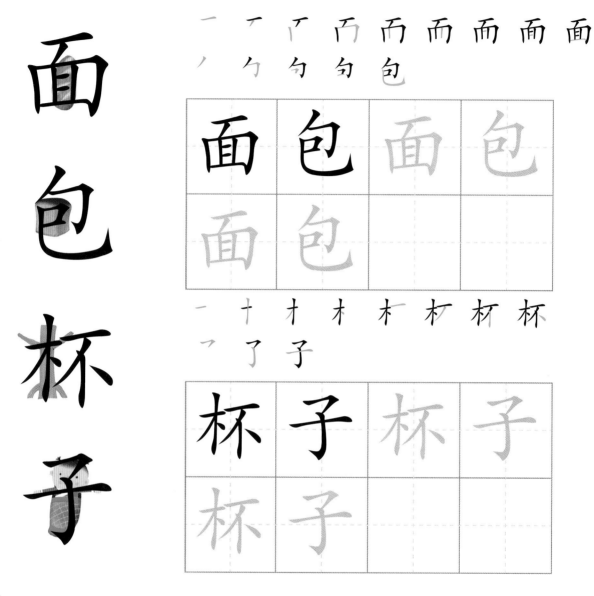

一 厂 厂 丙 而 而 面 面

⺈ 勹 勺 包

面	包	面	包
面	包		

一 十 才 オ 术 村 杯

⺈ 了 子

杯	子	杯	子
杯	子		

2 Write and say.

这是我们做的
___ ___，很好
吃！

在我的生日会，
我准备了纸___
___，大家一起
喝果汁。

3 Fill in the blanks with the correct words. Colour the hats using the same colours.

他们 好吃 面包 工作

我的爸爸在＿＿＿＿店＿＿＿＿，从星期一到星期六，他天天都很早起床去上班。

一天，爸爸带我去看他上班的地方。那里还有很多叔叔、阿姨，＿＿＿＿都会做＿＿＿＿，那些＿＿＿＿都很＿＿＿＿。

拼音输入法 Pinyin input

Number the sentences to make a meaningful paragraph. Then type the correct paragraph.

☐ 我们吃了炒饭、面条和饺子。

☐ 我觉得这家餐馆的饭菜很好吃，我还想去。

☐ 星期天，我们一家人去北京餐馆吃饭了。

☐ 我们还喝了果汁和蔬菜汤。

Cultures

1 Different cultures have different dining etiquettes. Learn some of the do's and don'ts in Chinese dining.

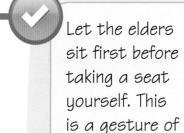

Let the elders sit first before taking a seat yourself. This is a gesture of politeness.

Let the elders eat first, or wait for them to say 'Let's eat.' before you start to eat. This is showing your respect for the elders.

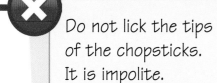

Do not lick the tips of the chopsticks. It is impolite.

Do not stick the chopsticks straight up in rice. It is not lucky.

Do not tap your rice bowl with chopsticks. It is a sign of begging for food.

2 Learn and practise how to use chopsticks. It is easy!

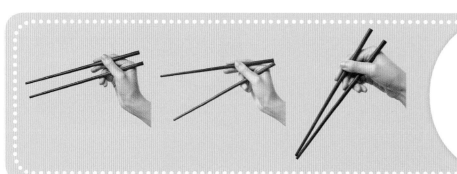

Hold the chopsticks in one hand. Use your index and middle fingers to move the upper stick up and down.

Project

1 Do you know how many tastes humans can sense? Learn about them.

Taste buds on our tongues are able to differentiate different tastes.

舌头
tongue

味蕾
taste buds

The sensation of taste includes five basic tastes:

甜 sweet

咸 salty

苦 bitter

鲜 umami

酸 sour

2 Try the blindfolded taste test with your friends and see whose tongue is more sensitive.

这是什么？

这应该是巧克力，它有一点儿苦，又有一点儿甜。

19

1 Look at the picture and draw your face in the blank circles. Write the characters. Role-play with your friends.

欢迎你来……

谢谢大家，我今天很高兴！

大家都有杯子、碗和筷子了吗？

你们渴吗？汽水从冰箱里拿来了。

今天的面条、炒饭和蔬菜汤看起来都很好吃。

你会不会写 bread 的中文字？

我最喜欢吃饺子了。

2 Work with your friend. Colour the stars and the chillies.

Words	说	读	写
面包	☆	☆	☆
面条	☆	☆	🌶
汽水	☆	☆	🌶
杯子	☆	☆	☆
渴	☆	☆	🌶
汤	☆	☆	🌶
冰箱	☆	☆	🌶
都	☆	☆	🌶
筷子	☆	🌶	🌶
炒饭	☆	🌶	🌶
饺子	☆	🌶	🌶

Words and sentences	说	读	写
准备	☆	🌶	🌶
餐馆	☆	🌶	🌶
欢迎	☆	🌶	🌶
碗	☆	🌶	🌶
同学们都准备了不同的美食。	☆	☆	🌶
这些都是我爸爸做的。	☆	☆	🌶

Talk about food and drinks	☆

3 What does your teacher say?

My teacher says ...

分享 Sharing

Words I remember

面条	miàn tiáo	noodle
面包	miàn bāo	bread
汽水	qì shuǐ	soft drink
杯子	bēi zi	cup, glass
渴	kě	thirsty
汤	tāng	soup
冰箱	bīng xiāng	refrigerator
都	dōu	all
筷子	kuài zi	chopsticks
炒饭	chǎo fàn	fired rice
饺子	jiǎo zi	dumpling
准备	zhǔn bèi	to prepare
餐馆	cān guǎn	restaurant
欢迎	huān yíng	to welcome
碗	wǎn	bowl

Other words

举行	jǔ xíng	to hold
美食节	měi shí jié	food festival
美食	měi shí	gourmet food
食物	shí wù	food
试	shì	to try
新鲜	xīn xiān	fresh
刀	dāo	knife
叉	chā	fork
盘子	pán zi	dish
哎呀	āi ya	oh (a kind of modal particle)
要	yào	to need, to want
舌头	shé tou	tongue
味蕾	wèi lěi	taste buds
甜	tián	sweet
咸	xián	salty
酸	suān	sour
苦	kǔ	bitter
鲜	xiān	umami

OXFORD
UNIVERSITY PRESS

Oxford University Press is a department of the University of Oxford.
It furthers the University's objective of excellence in research, scholarship,
and education by publishing worldwide. Oxford is a registered trade mark of
Oxford University Press in the UK and in certain other countries

Published in Hong Kong by
Oxford University Press (China) Limited
39th Floor, One Kowloon, 1 Wang Yuen Street, Kowloon Bay,
Hong Kong

Illustrated by Ah Lun, Anne Lee, Emily Chan, KY Chan and Wildman

Photographs for reproduction permitted by Dreamstime.com

China National Publications Import & Export (Group) Corporation is an authorized distributor of
Oxford Elementary Chinese.

Please contact content@cnpiec.com.cn or 86-10-65856782

ISBN: 978-0-19-082312-2

10 9 8 7 6 5 4 3 2